D1504988

HAMSTERS

BY KATHRYN STEVENS

The Child's World®

Published by The Child's World®
1980 Lookout Drive • Mankato, MN 56003-1705
800-599-READ • www.childsworld.com

Acknowledgments
The Child's World®: Mary Berendes, Publishing Director
The Design Lab: Design
Michael Miller: Editing
Sarah Miller: Editing

Photo Credits
© abalcazar/iStockphoto.com: 8; Aliaksandr Kazantsau/Dreamstime.com:
cover, 2, 6, 20 (food); EmiSta/iStockphoto.com: 4; emreogan/iStockphoto.
com: 5; Eric Wong/Dreamstime.com: 16; gisele/iStock.com: 3, 23 (toy); Han
Zhang/Dreamstime.com: 7; Haveseen/Dreamstime.com: 13; Igor Kovalchuk/
Shutterstock.com: cover, 1; Ingrid Prats/Dreamstime.com: back cover, cover, 2,
12 (wheel); Isselee/Dreamstime.com: 21; Kaikai/Dreamstime.com: 18; kone/
iStockphoto.com: 10; Ndjohnston/Dreamstime.com: 15; ozenli/iStockphoto.
com: 14; Papilio/Alamy: 11; PhotoDisc: 3, 22 (hamster), 24; Photographerv8/
Dreamstime.com: 17; Ruslan Kudrin/Dreamstime.com: 9; Verastuchelova/
Dreamstime.com: 19

ISBN: 9781631437281
LCCN: 2014959748

Printed in the United States of America
Mankato, MN
January, 2016
PA02297

NOTE TO PARENTS AND EDUCATORS

This Pet Care series is written for children who want to be part of the pet experience but are too young to be in charge of pets without adult supervision. These books are intended to provide a kid-friendly supplement to more detailed information adults need to know about choosing and caring for different types of pets. Adults can help youngsters learn how to live happily with the animals in their lives and, with adults' help and supervision, can grow into responsible animal caretakers later on.

CONTENTS

HAMSTERS AS PETS

Hamsters are cute little animals. They are very small and must be handled gently. Hamsters are lots of fun to watch—when they are awake! They sleep for most of the day. They are more active at night.

This girl is holding her hamster gently. Hamsters live for two or three years.

This dwarf hamster is extra small.

GOOD FOOD

Hamsters need foods that keep them healthy. Mostly they eat special hamster food. They also like fresh vegetables, cut up small. A little fruit is good, too. So is a little bit of egg or brown bread. Hamsters need plenty of clean water.

Hamster food is a mix of seeds, grains, and other things hamsters like to eat.

This hamster likes to sit in her food dish while she eats!

Hamsters like to live alone. Two hamsters in the same cage will fight.

A SAFE HOME

A hamster needs a clean, roomy cage.
There are many different kinds of cages.
Wire ones are good for climbing. Clear
tanks, or **aquariums**, also work well. Some
plastic cages have fun tunnels and hiding
spots. But they can be harder to clean.

Some dwarf hamsters do not mind living together.

A hamster's cage needs **bedding** on the bottom. The bedding should be changed every week. The hamster's bathroom area should be cleaned more often. The cage must have a hanging water bottle. The hamster needs a nest box for sleeping, too.

Hamsters love to put torn-up paper towels in their nests.

Shavings from aspen trees make great bedding. Hanging bottles like this one keep the hamster's water clean.

SOMETHING TO DO

Wild hamsters run around a lot, looking for food. They also dig and tunnel. Pet hamsters like to do these things, too. They enjoy running on exercise wheels. They love to climb ladders and crawl through tunnels. Pet stores sell toys that are safe for hamsters.

This hamster is running on an exercise wheel.

Paper-towel tubes make great hamster tunnels!

GOOD HEALTH

Exercise helps keep hamsters healthy. So does good food. Keeping their cages clean is important, too. Sometimes hamsters need to visit an animal doctor, or **vet**. Vets can often help sick hamsters.

Hamsters can carry germs, so handwashing is important. Very young children should not handle hamsters.

A vet is taking care of this sick baby hamster.

All hamsters need things to chew on. Their teeth grow all the time. Chewing keeps their teeth from getting too long. Hamsters like chewing on wood. Crunchy dog treats are good for chewing, too.

Hamsters love to chew on sunflower seeds.

Sometimes hamsters chew on their cages.

Hamsters like to snuggle close.

LOVING CARE

Hamsters need people who will take good care of them. Hamsters do not live as long as we may wish. But they are cute and fun. They do not mind being held gently by people they trust. They can make wonderful pets.

This hamster feels safe in her owner's hands.

NEEDS AND DANGERS

NEEDS:

- a nice, big cage
- clean bedding
- a nest box for sleeping
- hamster food
- other healthy foods
- a hanging water bottle
- safe things to chew
- an exercise wheel
- places to tunnel or climb

DANGERS:

- pine or cedar wood
- dogs and cats
- chewing soft plastics
- rough handling
- salty foods, sweets, or chocolate
- getting wet and cold
- strong sunlight

FUN FACTS

FUR:
Some hamsters have short, smooth fur. Others have long or fluffy fur.

SIZE:
Most pet hamsters are about 6 inches (15 centimeters) long.

EARS:
Hamsters have a good sense of hearing.

TAIL:
Hamsters have very short tails.

DWARFS:
Many dwarf hamsters are only 3 inches (8 centimeters) long.

SLEEP:
Hamsters can get grumpy if you wake them up during the day.

NOSE:
Hamsters have a great sense of smell.

GLOSSARY

aquariums (uh-KWAYR-ee-ums) Aquariums are clear tanks where animals can live.

bedding (BED-ding) Bedding for hamsters is something they can dig in on the bottom of their cage.

shavings (SHAY-vingz) Shavings are very thin pieces cut off of something.

vet (VET) A vet is a doctor who takes care of animals. "Vet" is short for "veterinarian" (vet-rih-NAYR-ee-un).

TO FIND OUT MORE

BOOKS:

Fox, Sue. *Hamsters.* Neptune City, NJ: T.F.H. Publications, 2006.

Ganeri, Anita. *Nibble's Guide to Caring for Your Hamster.* Chicago, IL: Heinemann Library, 2013.

Sjonger, Rebecca, and Bobbie Kalman. *Hamsters.* New York, NY: Crabtree, 2004.

Zobel, Derek. *Caring for Your Hamster.* Minneapolis, MN: Bellwether Media, 2011.

VIDEO/DVD:

Paws, Claws, Feathers & Fins: A Kid's Guide to Happy, Healthy Pets. Goldhil Learning Series (Video 1993, DVD 2005).

WEB SITES:

Visit our Web page for lots of links about pet care:
www.childsworld.com/links

Note to parents, teachers, and librarians: We routinely verify our Web links
to make sure they are safe, active sites—so encourage your readers to check them out!

INDEX

ABOUT THE AUTHOR
Kathryn Stevens has authored
and edited many books for young
readers, including books on animals
ranging from grizzly bears to
fleas. She's a lifelong pet lover and
currently cares for a big, huggable
pet-therapy dog named Fudge.